The Bulletproof Soul of a Poet

by

Robert H. Burke

WingSpan Press

Published in the United States and the United Kingdom
by WingSpan Press, Livermore, CA

The WingSpan name, logo and colophon are the trademarks of WingSpan Publishing.

ISBN 978-1-59594-993-6 (pbk.)
ISBN 978-1-59594-974-5 (ebk.)

First edition 2020

Printed in the United States of America

www.wingspanpress.com

1 2 3 4 5 6 7 8 9 10

Chapter One

The Happy Years

There are times in one's life, where the only thing left in life is memories of youth and laughter. When God blesses you with the most beautiful children in your World.

These Poems over time kept me alive, both physically and psychologically. I hope dear reader, that you may understand my time and dimension.

It is far too complicated and painful a story to tell herein, yet please know that these poems kept me alive with God's will.

Today, almost thirty years later, these poems are my salvation, and my prayers to thank God, and my Mother's memory in an effort to raise a child who honored her teachings of goodness and forgiveness.

Dear Mom on Mother's Day"

Mom. You were my world to me until 25 years ago
When the Lord saw you in the grace of your glow
Your commitment to a family through all of suffering
A beacon beyond human kindness, love's message of coveting
You faced every earthly obstacle with reverence and prayer
You suffered in silence for years, never resigned to despair
For the children were the pinnacles of your life's mission
And you never required or needed material possessions
Your life's fulfillment came from the highest of powers
Unique today in the world of human ivory towers
You were so different, so exceptional as a human being
No headstone's eloquent words can give your life meaning
I ponder the memories of God's true blessing today
Yet my anguish in missing your love grows everyday
I speak softly in prayer hoping my message is heard
Speaking the words, I barely said when you were of this earth
Mom, you too were my life, even more so as years pass
For I recognize your true beauty in reciting God's Mass
You were the spirit of goodness as spoken in the gospel
You practiced the Lord's divinity while others were hostile
You turned the other cheek; you felt the anguish of many

2

You brought happiness through the Lord to souls so empty
You filled the lives of relatives and friends with giving
Your memory is blessed everyday remembered in our living

All of My Love Everyday of Living
Your proud son,

Robert

"Journeys Taken"

May this journey today form a Bond of One's Heart
A spirit in strength never known to unravel
Ascending to Infinity, transforming The Depth of our Soul
A sadness for others who have never known being Whole
Never knowing the unspoken feelings comprised within Hearts
Love's True Warmth, True Purpose and Meaning
Our Destiny, our growth from a blossom, our sense of Being
A Friend, a Lover, a Companion So Giving
Life's True Worth, a United Partnership for Living

"Believe"

Believe that God has blessed you far beyond most of us
Believe that you are unique in Him so you will Trust
The words from the Angels, who speak to you everyday
For the message is clearly fulfilling your spirited way
He believes in you He loves you beyond a human being
He knows of your giving spirit, your passion in seeing
The goodness that life has to offer in your journey
Time is measured by goodness, the love of learning
Believe in Life, Believe in one's self everlasting
For He travels with you forever, for all eternity
He knows your contentment of heart within
He forgives your errors of way, all of our sins
So, travel His brightness, His guided path
And you shall believe in Him with a simple laugh
He has provided your spirit, your selfless giving
His Belief is that you Believe in truly Living

Believe in Him, and Love is eternal
Robert

"My Blessings of You"

As I think of all of my blessings
I walk far above the Earth with splendid glee
I thank the Lord for the sight of the magnificent sea
I thank Him exceptionally for His love of you and me
I see His kindness, his magical love within us
I know you are my human blessing, my ultimate trust
Within my loving embrace. I see His spirit's love
For you move me to a heaven felt from far above
I feel the angels' patience inspire my works, at its best
Where my love is so easily, yet magnificently expressed
It comes from within you when you touch me gently
When your smiling eyes consume my love, plentifully
I overflow with the splendor of your love's miracle
Sent to me from within Him, it is vastly empirical
To any love I have ever known within my living days
I want so much to express this wonder in so many ways
As I have believed from the very first day of finding you
We are very blessed with this God-given love, truly anew

You are My Loving Blessing
Robert

6

"Coming Home to My Sweet Child"

I brought you into your world on that special day
When angels trumpeted and choirs sang your Blessings
You blossomed from a seedling in such a magical way
While I watched you grow into such splendid dressings
The pride of My Love, I gave you on many days of play
I lived through you and with you for all this time
Never, ever forsaking your dreams, you fulfilled my spirit
Your journey emerged, happiness within your vigorous prime
You sacrificed for I, and the love for others, you could bare it
You sustained a special love within your poetry and rhymes
You traveled a righteous path, others could not understand why
Yet, I always knew you were well beyond others' belief in me
You followed my path without question, for I was your prince
I blessed you with special children for all they could truly be
You taught goodness and determination, the utmost of essence
You passed through the eye of the needle for the greater glory
Sustained by your love for human kindness so freely given
The chapters are written, the verses portrayed in life's story
Measured by life's vivid memories. Your passion for living
You are here now in my dimension, since your day of birth
Never, ever alone in your mind's eye and soul, renew our faith

Hope is always eternal, while you are here on our earth
You have truly blessed so many hearts, opened so many gates

Chapter Two

Parental Alienation Syndrome

This is a very difficult subject to discuss, as it is very personal, and haunts me to this very day. Thirty years have passed since my children were kidnaped from my life. Please understand that writing about this always brings me to tears, now at the age where life no longer matters, and I always revisit my Mom when I rehearse these poems to my children, when they were so vulnerable. I always believed that love would conquer all until there was no longer any hope.

Most people haven't a clue what Parental Alienation Syndrome is, and the media keeps it that way, because most of the perpetrators are in fact, Mothers who disrupt all visitation from Fathers, who want to see their children. And Mothers are usually the custodial parent and many a young child has suffered triggered psychological illnesses.

*"It includes a series of conscious programming techniques like "brainwashing" as well as subconscious and unconscious processes by the alienating parent combined with the child's own contribution denigrating the allegedly hated parent (Gardner, 1992) *1*

Expanding the Parameters of Parental Alienation Syndrome" *Glenn F. Cartwright*
<in00@musica.mcgill.ca>
Department of Educational Psychology and Counselling
McGill University
3700 McTavish
Montreal, QC H3A1Y2

Please cite as follows: *Cartwright, Glenn F. (1993) Expanding the parameters of parental alienation syndrome. American Journal of Family Therapy, 21 (3) 205-215*

"Truth of Love"

The instinct pervades, the history repeats

Memories close in time can bring such defeat

A measure of truth, of character, suspicion, distrust

The heart and emotions in conflict with trust

May honor prevail, gallantry persist

For there is more to love than history's list

A chance for the heart on its mission of mending

At peace in the belief that love, not fear, is never ending

Without the belief in the goodness of fellow man

The message of weakness draws a line in the sand

We must allow the passion of life to foster today

For God is providing a Spirit in guiding our way

We only need to believe in our measure of time

To deliver the ultimate message through love is sublime

"The Scales of Children's Justice"

Only old photographs to remember you by
Of wonderful times envisioned beside me where I lie
Sleeping of thoughts when life's goodness was proved
Can there be another life where the spirit in life is moved
To an uplifting of Justice, where the truth is pursued
Without the loss of One's love for her mother
Is it all possible, a dichotomy with one another
Will it descend upon the emotional turmoil of youthful faith
In the messenger of a rearing adult, a shivering quake
Exiled in an emerged pyre to purge one's sins
Of a trust and respect reexamined where no one wins
Forgiveness of transgressions, reunion of compassion
Although black robes of Justice and political factions
Cannot come to grips with the emotional turmoil
That is created for Children, Love becomes foiled
With the intervention to exile One's Fatherhood Rights
Where Dollars replaced Parenting via Big Brother's Might

"Graduation Congratulations Laura"

I remember the first day of nursery school
How you looked forward to meeting new children
When you made friends so easily with your beaming smile
How proud you made me as a Daddy, as a human being
I remember your spirit of brightness as you lit up the school
Your possession for intrigue, your curiosity in full bloom
I remember your doing homework at the kitchen table
Seeing your wonderment with learning and having a gift
In discovering knowledge with a passion of a future scholar
I remember the hours of joy with your favorite rhymes
Of searching for Goldbug secretly hiding within each story
I remember your first poem to Grampa as he entered Heaven
The short story you wrote about Daddy brought me to tears
I have read this Father's Day story every year for ten years
Knowing you would seek the highest plateau you endeavored
I knew you had a gift; a remarkable insight reaching horizons
Beyond what most people will accomplish in one's life
You have reached the first plateau on the way to the summit
You will find the next traverse more challenging, more fulfilling
Yet, your vision will provide you strength of conviction
To attain individuality within this world where life will lead you

You will have a wonderful place of influence amongst many
You will discover your uniqueness of Human Spirit

May God Bless Your Future Journey in Life
Love & Affection
Dad

"Life's Blessings"

Touched by a heartbeat, blossoms this unique human being

From the seedlings of angels, a special child is born

Touched by the miracle of creation for all humanity to see

Where eloquent words cannot describe the emotions adorned

Touched by the joy of sharing, life's trust is treasured

A cherub's unconditional love is so freely given

A key to unlocking the meaning of love, life's purpose measured

Touched by the anointing of Joseph's blessing, a spirit forever

Touched by the measure of life, God's awakening by a child

We share a special child, our consummated blessing

"God's Strength for Fatherhood"

My sunlight was cast aside during the past few years
When my children were taken away from me in tears
For bitterness and scorn, for the sake of divorce
Left my beautiful babies helpless during the actions and course
The courts of Justice with blindness for all its effects
It's system portraying a justice of alleged suspects
Without regard to the benefit, the rights of Fatherhood
Lost in a system of due process. As a statue of petrified wood
Could feel no loss of compassion, of love in true need
For innocent children to be despaired by a mother's deed
In destroying the bond, the giving of a loved one
Forever, a travesty, casting aside the new morning sun
We battle the unforgiving magistrate, we know as the law
To overcome all obstacles, to protect a defense we all saw
Unsympathetic darkness. never knowledge to the light of day
God gives us strength and the fortitude for forgiving ways
No matter the wounds and scars, through sacrifice of lambs
The love of such radiance and spirit, God gently hold our hand
With God's Grace and salvation, we will again be together
For the Love of one's Children is blessed in God's spirit forever

"God's Power Through Angels and Doves"

Where have the days gone, the truth along with them
Replaced by the prayers to God, words from my pen
Traveling the Book of Job, God is all that is left
Prayers keep my soul alive. While my heart feels death
I await the day of forgiveness the truth be it told
Belief in the goodness of souls, family past I behold
A remembrance of love, and the innocence it projects
Seeking the goodness in man, Children He protects
Are taken from my heart, yet the memories linger
The touch of one's hand, my face searched by baby's fingers
How far a distance can they penetrate hatred's fences
An iron will must be displayed or tears will never cease
Never lost faith in Jesus, stand another day, never retreat
For these precious gifts, God has freely given to me in love
Children of heritage, a peace from God's flight of the Dove
The journey has been so long Dear Lord, spirit renewed
Over many years of discontent, consciousness in light reviewed
I beseech you My God, let my strength be You're blessing
To reach the pinnacle of the mountain's crest, never resting
Until my reason for living has been concluded with Love
My precious Angels rejoining my life, the flight of the Dove

"What If"

What if life could be different for you, my children
And I was there, every day of your daily lives
What if God could bring us together, a Family once again
Would such a miracle take place, is this the hope inscribed
What if I could touch your heart and enter your spirit renewed
In God's Loving Grace providing a path to being at your side
What if I could visit you only in dreams, a loving place review
A moment within your vision would bring the joy of all pride
What if I could share your joy and ease your heart of pain
I would give all of my moments remaining for such hope
Enlightened, restored with humanity, alive with breath to cope
What if the days pass as age forgets the image of love's way
Lost over priorities of daily life, families of one's importance
What if you finally have the courage to search our lost bond
Will mother be willing to fulfill your wish to seek the chance
What if life offered a new beginning to love and be loved
Where a sense of childhood is not too late to revisit innocence
What if your wish was granted, our prayers for others forlorn
Would we recapture the moments of a child's love of true poems
What if you knew the truth, I would give my life for you both
Nor your belief of a Father's absence lost in jurist catacombs

What if you knew the truth of my heart and soul's yearning
To be a loving Father whose heart you both have always owned
What if you had always known my emotions, the true learning
A Heart seeking journey, God to finally bring you Home

A Sincerely Loving Dad

"God and His Child's Faith"

I see the vision of hazy mist encapsulating our seashore

Where once the flow of tide of musing thoughts resounded

The cliffs of stone turned to sandcastles in the sea's wake

Where once nature's love embraced its natural elements

The coarseness of grains of sand burned my senses

Where once its warmth and softness enveloped my spirit

The crest of waves marks time with life's cadence

Where once it marked the peace of the mind's pace

The dunes are now my desert of protective refuge

Where once the echoes of children laughing were cherished

The sound of seagulls screeching for their daily sustenance

Where once Jonathan graced the beach in flight for all to view

I hear Jonathan cry to God as the Great White taunts him

Where once I felt God would finally answer my only prayer

The mist of an uncertain journey clouds the memory

Where once a righteous path of natural law would be pursued

Yet changing colors of God's Rainbow can be renewed

Where once storms took upon many dimensions at sea

I traveled through the desert too long to give unto despair

For once I remember the memories of a child's faith

Beyond the anguish a living creature must endure

The mist of uncertainty escapes from the seashore of one's mind
Where once again God's seashore creates peace and tranquility

Love,
Dad

"Sit in reverie, and watch the changing colors of the waves that break upon the idle seashore of the mind"
Henry Wadsworth Longfellow

"Love on Laura's 15th Birthday" (1998)

My heart awakens writing poems to you
Especially when words are sent, ever so true
Wishing I could celebrate your Birthday today
Holding your photograph, moments of joy from yesterday
Remembering a Father's Love beyond comprehension
Long ago, so many years lost without mention
Beyond words said through our poetic vision
A bond so strong, never denied a heart's religion
I pray for the day of being together in future birthdays
No man writes alone without inspiration of prayers
For a Birthday of unification of love's presence
In a person to touch our heart and soul's pure essence

All of my Love on your Birthday.
Dad

"Kristina's Valentine" (1998)

Cupid has a special Day
He's sending a message of Love
From My Heart, more than words can say
A special flight of doves
Take wings in clear direction
In clear site of God's protection
Our destiny we accept with humility
Love's strength and emotional collection
Of memories past, and hope for the future
A Love so profound, no matter the reflection
Thoughts are always in the strength of our bond
My Love always and forever ever so profound

Love Always.
Dad

"Laura's Valentine" (1998)

Love from the Heart
I so freely give
While we are apart
Vivid memories live
On this special day
When cupid appears
Showing me the way
To visualize Teddy Bears
Dancing and Singing
Protecting life's fears
And frailties of human beings
Love has blessed us everyday
Teddy Bears will show the way
On this Valentine's Day

Love Always and Forever.
Dad

"Love to Laura and Kristina" (Christmas 1998)

Evergreens, mistletoe, and the Nutcracker Soldier

Remind me of days gone by, years growing older

I envision the Doves of Peace, the Angel's protection

Are upon you both, the symphony abounds with reflection

Of memories of wonder, a scent of merriment's treasure

To Dream of My Daughters, my one remaining pleasure

I reminisce of teddy bears, satin and colored bows

And dreams of enchantment, a winter wonderland show

The spirit of love, eternity's candle. The warmth rekindles

Its embrace of innocence, heart's sincerity never dwindles

In the measurement of time, the distance of paternity

For My Love for you both is for all of eternity

All My Love
Dad

"Birthdays Apart"

I sit here in my sense of isolation

Attempting to see you again, results of effort forlorn

I think of memories of years past

Of pleasantry in smiles, warm and affectionate hugs

I can even sense the smell of your hair beneath my chin

You were both all my world, as you are now in my dreams

But I was present in person then, desolate now

I feel you think of me as abandoned without feelings inside

A Heart so trembling, a strength no longer consuming

Seeking a purpose in life, God give me strength today

As tears of these memories aged a once youthful spirit

For you brought me such strength within your love

A dependence and security in your vision of Dad's future

I have tried so many, many times to reach out to you again

To touch your imagination and spirit in memories of dreams

To assure you both that my spirit of love will never die

So, please dream of me as I feel your hearts today

My love is undiminished as the day you were born

"The Distance of Love"

Too many days dreaming of soft breezes and warm sands
Wishing for flight from my dilemma in reaching your hands
Care taking souls, my inner most spirit truly beholds
Love and friendship with my children as extended life unfolds
Awakening to the remembrance of past together, life so sublime
Protecting my children as the future appeared so defined
Pray for forgiveness for past transgressions, to begin life anew
A place where our love and compassion are the essence of truth
The meaning of life together is the dove's peace and tranquility
In flight of God's artistry, strength of love's profound ability
To overcome all obstacles life may bring in the future
In strength of commitment as a family, we will be blessed
Within God's Grace, I have both of you in my life forever
The height and breath of our love will never diminish
Until the angels take me, and life on earth is finished

"Before I Sleep, Prayers of Hope"

I have missed you, my Darlings, Laura and Kristina

Always in my heart, my thoughts, my spirit forever

In strength of oceans and tides, in depth of fathoms

I seek your faces, offering peace and tranquility

The touch of your hands, the capture of your embraces

Never leaves my senses throughout the years of life

Although circumstances beyond our control keeps us apart

My heart always feels you both so near to me

Especially when I drift through memories while alone

I love you both, Laura and Kristina, more than life

When I am morose and dispirited, your image brings me life

Helps me in my prayers to seek a guiding life for our future

When we will once again be together, peaceful sleep reality

For now, dearest children, dream sweetly, may angels guide you

Sweet melodies, soft poems bring reassurance into the night

Visions of splendor, memories of goodness at morning's light

Goodnight my precious children, I am with you both tonight

"The Message of Love to My Children"

The distance that separates us while we are apart

Transcends the spirit. our love from the heart

The images of our bonding, the strength our love

A flight of song, remembering the pure flight of Doves

A peace I find when thoughts of you both suddenly appear

To move me from the turmoil, whose presence is so near

My dreams unfold, mesmerizing God's beautiful faces

To touch your hand, the vision of happier places

Where safety and trust were within a Father's arms

Providing a Father's protection from all earthly harm

Knowing the pain would subside with a hug and a kiss

Gentleness and caring, daddy's comforting never remiss

I pray for a unity, such a long journey through spirit anew

For a Father's commitment of love for his children is true

In a world where others may decide a child's fate of love

God hears my prayers of anguish, absent of Children of life

His glorious spirit will serve me through obstacles of strife

He shall grant me serenity and vision to amend the wrongs

Of Children lost within a system perpetuating a woman scorned

Dearest Laura,

I had a dream the other night, we were both together once again

It was the beginning of the end of the world, as we knew it to be. And, The Lord was descending upon the earth in our final days.

As we were preparing for our journey to life everlasting.

The Lord showed us a new world in Heaven, days before our journey.

Heaven was beyond belief of human eyes, human thoughts or human senses.

The colors of the landscape were beyond human comprehension.

We looked to the horizon in heaven and the stars covered the heaven's galaxies.

And, then I saw the brightest star of all descend to just above our souls,

When I recognized the same brightness of warmth I had only felt once before.

I had whispered to this star's appearance on the first evening of your birth.

As He knew God sent this star to me on the most blessed day of my life. The Birth Day of the brightest star of my life.

All My Love,

Laura's 17th Birthday, September 20, 2001   Dad

"The Pawns in The Chess Game"

Children so innocent, knowing only love and affection
From two people once giving, known as Mom & Dad
See thorns where roses were once cherished
See thorns of hurt, pain and desolation
An impact so devastating, youth removed from the cocoon
"It's not fair," stated by an innocent child
Becoming the pawn of possession, innocence gone
The littlest one, not of the age to grasp the impact
Of revenge of a mother, a woman scorned
They only know that Daddy is no longer around
He grasps for what is the birthright of all children
To know love of both parents, unconditional, most sound
In his heart of love to convey, no children are to blame
The age of innocence, and learning the meaning of love
should be the only purpose in the restoration
the feeling of goodness, once felt without pain
No, "it's not fair," the courts of jurisprudence shouldn't allow
the benefits of children submerged, over Lawyers' shame
the impetus of money, possession, pride and blame
Forgiveness should be tantamount in keeping spirits high
For it is the children who hurt, separated from family ties

That bonded and secured the imagination of goodness
A life's impact, faith and security are forever gone

"Justice for The Insect- Extermination"

The insect lives an auspicious life in the Underground world
Below nature's giant world of power and illumination
Except, beware of the field mice patrol lurking its nose within
The safe haven of home, scenting the pleasure carnivorous siege
Without backbone, the army of rodents mount a vicious attack
Volatile pursuit, virile soldiers' spittle uncontrollable virulence
Conquest is law of nature's domain, stature in scale, servile
Brought before King Rat's tribunal, ravenous appetite awaits
The thorns of the rosebush below, nourishment be punishment
Its nectar of sustenance can't contain remedy to insignificance
The sinewy Oak Tree contains many insignificant such as I
Yet the fire ants of our nation protect the Oaks strength
Disorderly and contemptuous are these members of community
For the oak is the feeding ground of fleshy bark by millions
Fire in the belly of the Oak, while seasons change elements
Yet the roots sprout in many directions in earth's sun and sky
Leaving rodents and serpents to tunnel the secret channels
One floor of Earth just below a place appropriate, Dante's Inferno

"The Love for a Child"

It is unquestioned, unconditional, a gift from the Heavens

To have breathed in God's Spirit, to have witnessed a miracle

In the birth of magic, the touch of God's Hand

To be so deserving, to be blessed with security

Enriched, empowered toward the future of growth

Of an angel from a fallen star, to a Cherub in full flight

Watching pure innocence, the sense of dependence grows

We believe in the true sense of life's purpose

A long-awaited message to amend life of wrongfulness

Bringing the traditional sense of worth to the sublime

An undefined Love, a bonding forever, for all time

On God's Good Earth, an abundance of Faith

In Life's true meaning, The Love for a Child

"Days of Hope & Despair"

My mind fears the darkness, the invasion of gloom
Determined to see God's Light, a vision in bloom
How does one's heart hope for the best
Of human understanding, compassion put to the test
A child's blessing, imagination of childhood developing
Missing magic unfolding, precious growth enveloping
I've missed these many precious years, lost for one's spite
Once there was love and affection, children's smiles of delight
As a father watched over and protected their dreams
Of safety and security, teddy bear protection, comfort in means
All faded into darkness, a nightmare of people in robes
Representing justice, sacrificial lamb on behalf of the probe
To administer the verdict of extradition, the system's scorn
Where warmth and caring of one's father is never considered
Only jewels of possession displayed within political glitter
Stand in the way of happiness and the goodness of a child
Lost in the scorn as a wife's affidavits of deceit are filed
Disregarding the welfare of daughters' emotional damage
The process continues over years of loneliness and fear
Testing sanity, one's spirit and dignity with a vengeance
Leaving the blessing of Laura and Kristina to God

Chapter 10
From "Poems & Letters from Deadbeat Daddy"

"Although I was not being allowed telephone contact with Laura and Kristina, I always sent letters, poems, and personal greeting cards, knowing full well, that Barbara was destroying every shed of communication. By this time, this behavior of destruction by Barbara was going on for 3 years."

"The Price of Vindictiveness"

Who will save your soul, will you feel your folly

Does the scorn give you peace, a sense of power

Can regret be felt, or is hate controlling the hurt

Do you understand the lives affected, the love lost

Where teddy bears live nightmares, darkness envisioned

Is the soul worth saving, life now worth living

Who else will truly care when the future chapters written

The effects of remorse, regret, sympathy for the devil

Cannot save yourself when the Soul is not willing

Will the battle won bring you glory you so desire

Will the wine and song temper the fire

The flame of contempt on behalf of revenge

Piercing the mind with migraine psychic revenge

The soul cannot live in such an environment

Where forgiveness and acceptance of a Child's innocence

Can never recapture the soul's creative goodness

Only demons take homage from such a discipline

Who will save your soul when nothing else matters

On the way through Universe travel. Life's final day

Through the microcosm of the terrestrial angels' gate

Or the Devil's due within the place of fate

The legacy of lost souls will live to see tomorrow

Through the torment and pain left for others to bare

Where precious lives will be devastated by a woman's scorn

Sacrificing the Souls of Youth, a casket mourned

Souls of so many lost in a future generation

For the Soul that could not be saved for the greater glory

"Freedom of Justice, The Righteous Hypocrite"

The book of statues is overwhelmed with crimes
Committed by law abiding citizens considered in times
Where social stigma attacks its fangs to constitutional maligns
From adultery, sexual privacy, child support are felony crimes
Criminalizing legal notions, yet rape in some states is blind
Cynicism and hypocrisy of law of conduct is criminalized
Laws enacted based solely on a group's personal morality
Would certainly be time better spent on predatory criminality
Courts will never set matters right, so comes legislature's might
Enacting laws, posturing the popular belief, not what is real
Justice is now served by the righteous vote without appeal
To a country of citizens whose heritage is the Bill of Rights
Has been lost in a country where laws are enacted with might
In a secular, heterogeneous society impacting politicians
Wrapping themselves in the banner of false patriotism
While Americans' concern in general is need for materialism
We have forgotten to relish our rights of Freedom and Liberty
Secure in our sense that intangible beliefs are here for eternity
A citizen no longer has to visit our nations distant borders
To see the challenges from the chains of tyranny and order
I have faced firsthand, its desecration within its infirmary

Within a prison, the symbol of crime is imprisonment

A bastion of drugs and alcohol, resolutions wrongly envisioned

A tool of justice, punishment reigned by a political movement

Where Justices recuse Responsibility of Oath for social cause

In bargaining for dollars influenced by financial calculus

Where Children suffer from the absence of Love, manipulation

In honor of political right, social truth via incarceration

While the district attorney keeps political ambitions alive

Held without a Constitutional Bail, falsified affidavit supplied

Quotas are provided to the News Media Public Image

Propagandizing while Constitutional Rights are maligned

Rights have no place in the eyes of politicians, judges' merits

In deciding a case from the evidence of facts presented

For the media and politicians may react with resentment

The Greatest Injustice, Children's Right are truly ignored

A Father is illegally removed from Child's Life, never deplored

As the Law matters for nothing, while the righteous all deny

Swaying the presumption of innocence to guilty without trial

As prosecuting and defense attorneys decide fate in collusion

Where the political media influence imparts public delusion

In pre-conceived opinions of disgust and disdain

Wanting vengeance based solely on untruths, innuendo & pain

There is no right of defense, fairness of documented fact

So too is lost my belief in the Canon of Jurisprudence impact

The conclusion of law, where a System of Justice absolved

The pain of the disenfranchised falsely accused is ever resolved

God bless you, should you be a victim of Political Blacklisting

Controversy over issues of law will be ignored, priorities missing

From the Scales of Justice, replaced by character assassination

As the cause of the Legal Pulpit is beyond Ostracization

Let me arise and open the gate
To breathe the world's warm air along the beach
And, to let love in, and let out the hate
And anger at living with the scorn of fate
To let in life, and let out death
To be grateful for my strength in faith
For the gardeners who have blossomed
The seeds of nurture and love's soul
A harmony between one's soul and life
People who make us happy with peaceful giving
Who have lived introspectively with inner-serenity

A Joyous and Blessed Christmas
With friendship,
Robert

"Bring Peace to My Heart Children"

I wish my love could move telepathically

Through blue skies and star lit tapestry

Where a simple kiss could touch like a breeze

And tides could tingle your toes on sandy shores

When the sun's warmth could embrace your hugs

Sometimes, my mind can envision such things

But my heart can so easily transform into tears

Where the drops could fill the ocean's crest

In a tidal wave of the fury of a storm's surge

When the clouds must so easily envelop your hearts

In the loneliness we share, the emotional message

Consuming my day's activities, my life is missing

The years of memories of peace, not since then

When life was so worth every precious day living

Has been taken away for so long now, only memories linger

Yet distance now, as the senseless war in Vietnam

Where the war of thorns and broken promises

Has caused you children, so much undeserved pain

A martyr in your mind, a non-physical presence

Where love, hugs and a commitment were shared

From past days, so long ago, now a repressed vision

I've lost all of natural worth, yet it does not matter
The greatest loss in all my life is not sharing your love
Yet my soul has traveled to ask for your forgiveness
To move in spirit, God's blessing your kindness
Bringing hearts together in time, once again in peace
Let our world of nature spring eternal with love

"My Daughter
There are many things
I want for you
So many wishes in my heart
As I watch you grow into your own life
And leave your childhood behind. . . .
I wish you the strength
To face the challenges with confidence,
Along with the wisdom
To choose your battles carefully. . . .
I wish you the world
Of adventure and experience,
And also, the serenity
That comes from listening
To your inner voice
As the world rushes
Around you. . . .
I wish you the satisfaction
Of seeing your goals achieved,
And also, the true contentment
That is born of simple things. . . .
Moments caught and cherished.
And my greatest wish

Is that you will always remember
How much you are loved....
For you are a beautiful, special person....
A woman I am proud
To have for a daughter

All My Love & Affection
Dad
Author: Jennifer Fujita (Hallmark Cards)

Sent to Kristina on June 12, 2001, after a previous card and personal poem entitled "God and His Child's Faith," sent certified mail, return receipt requested was returned. The prior poem was sent on May 10, 2001.

CHAPTER THREE

Love Found, Love Lost

There is a psychological makeup where one believes that love conquers all. In my life, the opposite was true, where the trust in love was always proven to be suspect, as for some reason I was attracted to women, who had psychological scars in their very own lives, usually an outgrowth of childhood abuse, or marriage abuse, both physically and psychologically. The exception was the youthful girls, from a different era, where families were the focus of support and goodness with not a lot of trauma in these sweet girl's lives.

Childhood was far different in the 1950's and 1960's, almost all children had a Mother and a Father, and many relatives, as an extended family, where almost everyone took an interest in every child's life, and shared in the upbringing of all children. And, neighbors were also involved via sports activities. In my case it was CYO baseball, local sports, etc.
People were always involved in the local neighborhood community, where if a neighbor was wealthier than your family, you would be helped quietly without the child's knowledge, as the neighborhood had been doing so for many generations that inherited these same principles of goodness. The neighborhood mentored you, from grade school teachers to nuns and priests, even a Speaker of the House of Representatives, Tip O'Neil who lived in one of my neighborhoods. Older kids took an interest in you, as you were a friend of one brother or sister, and they taught life's lesson to the younger kids to avoid.

The neighborhood covered many small streets, a ballpark next to a wooded area containing a reservoir, and woods, a 9 hole golf course and a local grammar school with an outside basketball court, which also was used for dancing once a year, and marching bands would come for Veteran's parades, and Saint Lucia events where Mother Mary would be adorned with streams of money to donate to the local community.
Once we became a society of mobility and transitioned to a global economy, everything changed as to the family unit, and neighborhoods, and we became of transitional society.

Today, for the most part, we no longer have roots, where a sense of security exists.
And, because of the need for financial security, we have become a nation of financial insecurity, where we no longer trust in the system where the future is bright.

It is no longer an issue of family, but survival for most neighborhoods, all because approximately forty years ago, opportunities curtailed for a global economy that has been besmirched by our elected leaders and corporations profit margins, without any recognition of the people in the trenches of America Corporate Structure Hierarchy.

What I have learned over these forty years, is that most families have so much pressure upon them, where emotions run high, and securities low, that anger takes hold within the family structure, the basic premise that anger is manifested via abuse. Yes, this abuse has been a learned behavior, usually by men, but often by women via psychological traumas, where the abuse of a Father from years ago, becomes predominant in a current situation.

Yet, as often done within a system of government, is for overreaction, for a quick solution, via courts, police, and politicians where the system is used to file false claims, fully supported by the media, where issues are sensationalized for attention, rather than understanding the details of the dimension and how to actually correct the issue, and to understand that some people will use the system to punish an innocent person, what I call boilerplate dictates. Research has hardly been accomplished as to many issues. It is all about the quick solution, rather than understanding the intricate details of humans.

The repercussions and aftereffects of abuse are devastating to those who love the victim, and almost every one of my lovers and friends carry the devastating consequences for most of life without any therapy of which many victims refuse such therapy at all. And, it carries over into every relationship the victim endures, and a trust is always suspect.

"God's Cathedral"

The naturalist poets displayed God's blessings upon us
With magnificent gifts of His earth's true trust
His creatures of plains and mountains of serenity
Falls and rivers' majesty, God's Mystery divinity
A geological temple painted by His fingertips
Pleasuring the human heart with tranquility
Lands destined for human's destructive destiny
Saved by men of God, who knew heavenly dressings
Envisioned here on earth for common blessings
For human symbols of worship at God's altar
Touched the soul's deepest sanctuary in prayer
Our National Monuments of God's Paintbrush

With Loving Friendship

Robert

"How I Found My Love"

It has been so rare to love, truly in my life

My obsession to please fought within the demons of strife

I believed I could live life without a woman within

As I had for so many years, I could never win

The heart of another's full understanding, I hid away

Until one beautiful night, I found you embraced my feelings

Never felt in so long, I was consumed, confused, reeling

Those nights we drifted upon the sea's waves enveloped us

Blissful caresses, soft tender kisses, the pleasure and lust

I doubted my feelings, inner adequacies pervaded my mind

Did I deserve such a splendid gift from you, I was blind

We became a union of comfort and joy, yet fear remained

I could not deserve such love, only having known pain

Deserving alone, I could not give what I had not attained

It had been my history of acceptance, God's fulfillment

And He provided me sustenance and a loving commitment

I thought I would return to a life of oneness without you

Yet each time you left my life, I was unable to exist or renew

My thoughts of you repeated in such wonderful dreams

Remembrances of tenderness, compassion, and love beamed

No one had ever given me such joy as Mom's Love

I learned a valued lesson, as a gift from above

And I know I will only know true love with you

My folly, my mistakes has hurt your truth in our love

I have realized there can be no desire for love if not your love

Until my days have drifted away and God consumes my spirit

"Recognizing True Love"

True Love is so easily recognized
The soft touch within one's vision
The smile of contentment and peace
The spirit of youth and charm revisited

Love is hearing the words expressed
Feeling its warmth sensually
Seeing it professed within actions
Touching its very core of existence

Everlasting love never loses its luster
As every moment is always at capacity
Every day a newness of meaning
Knowing the moment within eternity

When two spirits become intwined
And fit so very perfectly divine
When eyes meet eyes in heaven
One within the spirit is well defined

"Just When You Think"

Just when you think life has become so mundane
Her vision appears as the light of God's new day
She captures your heart effortlessly, in so many ways

Just when you know, you have seen enough pain
Her eyes lift you spirit far-beyond simple ways
She raptures your soul with a very new day

Just when you give into despair without a thought of refrain
Her voice of reassurance speaks of sunlight, not rain
She captures your life with her soft reassuring way

Just when your love of mankind comes into question again
Her words of sensual love whispers hope, not disdain
She enamors your goodness, as if a child at play

Just when you believe her life is a blessing without bane
Her spirit transcends the earth to my heavenly stay
She opens my mind and heart's joy, forever and a day

"Our First Date"

My first date with the woman who captured my heart

Makes me feel a charmed man without any regret

I will write this poem with a champagne toast

I shall feel of all the men in her life I may mean the most

You see, she allured me beyond words of my vivid imagination

She smiled from afar from the across the bar with infatuation

I never expected to seek her, I was just a man having a drink

Yet, I approached her with warmth that I no time to think

She said her breathtaking hello, I began living a dream

I had set within writing scenes, just feeling the verse

She was so alive, a scene of God's reality, no time to rehearse

She was the one I had always needed during years of strife

I cared that she knew I was different from others in her life

My heart and mind sensitized beyond anything felt before

All my years on God's Good Earth, she knew me beyond allure

So natural the chemistry, so thrilling the feelings of lust

I prayed this wonderful night would never, ever leave us

I have been blessed beyond human kindness and love's meaning

Tonight, I am in heaven with a woman where I am dreaming

I pray the Lord keeps the dreams alive where love is enhanced

Intimacy's profound sharing God's touch, our intimate dance

"When We Dance"

When we dance, I enter the gates of Heaven

I feel the softness of clouds, the light of God

I hold you within my embrace, heavenly driven

By love and the comfort of your sweet sigh

We travel together to a far different world

We see our earth as our own and we laugh

Observing others so lost within the search

A search, not many travel with such a spirit of love

For us it is as natural as the sunrise upon the earth

Our music may be of tides, the waves flowing within

Of diamond speckles upon heightened sand dunes

The lyrics of song from plovers and terns' speech

Of parasail's directing love's message by the wind

Your happiness felt within all of my senses

For I dance to the song of life we now embrace

Affaire d'amour affaire du Coeur

Robert

"Thoughts of Our Love"

This wonderful day begins with my thoughts of love for you

Knowing that this evening we will love again, de je vous

I will travel to your haven with such lustful anticipation

Needing every ounce of your love within your destination

I hear songs of bliss, I can taste your heavenly kiss

I see within those magical eyes, the love I so miss

Stories will be told, magical moments remembered

Love will be in abundance, lust within the embers

Long after we have captured all of our senses

Feeling your soul deep within, so very pensive

I shall want only you within my embrace

Finding my lips softly kissing your face

Cuddling against the shape of your torso

Cupping your breasts as my loins quiver so

The softness of clouds' travel my fingers

As we know our warmth always lingers

Deep within our love, splendor exudes

For this love is forever, ever so true

Amour, tombe' des nues/ Love fallen from the clouds, Robert'

"Love's True Unfolding Journey"

I visualize my arms enveloping you within the softness of water
Caressing the voice of God's blessed tide so near to our senses
As His moon and stars captured our hearts as one, forever

I now carry the peace that I felt within your heavenly kiss
Far different than my many prior years of living without you
I felt the serenity of true goodness without feeling ordinary

As you held my embrace as an everlasting and loving testament
Of youthful days of laughter and the remembering goosebumps
A rebirth of imaginary dreams of splendor as when a child

My heart fluttered, as I tasted your warm body within me
As my breath consumed all of my energy, love's true divinity
God provided His consummated, enlightening passage to life

For you captured every fiber of my human existence's entirety
On that splendid evening within our only destination in life
The wine of love consumed me with the poets' laurels of history
All the Love within me   Robert

Love's Testament
"God has smiled upon us with Love"

I thought of this moment, anticipating the hours

Here within our love nest, hope you like the flowers

I thought this poem for many days with many a wish

Expressing my deepest love and affection, never remiss

For loving you is so magical, so wonderfully alluring

Looking in your eyes with all of your lust, just so adoring

Such beauty, such passion within our folding embrace

Where we find the pleasures of love and lust so encased

Within our sensuous minds we love for many hours

We are meant to know such pleasures, the scent of flowers

Our soft tender kisses send such flavors of love's taste

Where my Aphrodite opens her pillars of love's wait

I consume her Goddess's warmth within her whole being

Finding her treasure of love, the pleasures I am seeing

I look upon her smile, and her beautifully lustful eyes

As she nourishes my being within the heat of her fire

She consumes every moment, I see her pleasure's desire

Stroking me with her taste of my silk's hardness of loins

I cannot breathe as her love's passion is completely enjoyed

Our hearts beat in synch, I move to her soft pink peaks

She places my love within her chalice, I lovingly beseech
We have entered the gates of eternal love and bliss
Where nothing else matters except for all of this
For this love is so different than others we have known
Where our passion and tenderness will never be forlorn
It is far too precious a gem, this love's precious stone

Annuit coeptis a' point avec d'amour
"God has smiled upon us with Love"
Robert'

"We Live the Loving Words of Poets"

All my words of symbolic love for you
Merely touch the surface of my view
Of what life is with you in review
Shakespearian description wouldn't do

I love you as much as natural breathing
Beyond the earth and all the seasons
Far above all mysteries, of holy reasoning
My love is so substantial with your pleasing

Cannot fathom life without our loving sweet kisses
I cannot see the world your great heart elicits
Unless you are within my heart's many a bliss
Seeking all of your love, so very delicious

Once upon a time, begins our love every day
I can write poetic words in such a profound way
For our love is measured by my heavenly stay
Knowing that your heart is never far away

To be so deserving of knowing your true love

Knowing Irish poets could not measure from above
Such words of love, of devotion, a healing suave
Soothing all afflictions of the lonely heart

I am blessed for such love you so profess
I am you're loving wordsmith, I must confess
Who lives his life with this love no less
Than the prayers of children, never repressed

I cannot state enough such love and desire
For my words will flow until life expires
Yet, I will know I have consumed the fire
Of passion, of love's truth of words we so require

With all of the passion of Our Love, within us
Your Loving Poet,
Robert'

"This Day, a Wish"

May today be blessed within your heart
Your subliminal thoughts of love a part
Of celebration from it's very brilliant start

Make today a journey in awakening all senses
From your inception at birth uniquely extensive
To me, you have magically made love pensive

Hard to accomplish in this day and age's time
Yet, you always see and understand human rhyme
And obstacles are merely challenges in our mind

Your spirit unique, your kindness in giving of self
Cannot usually be found in novels of spirit's wealth
Yet, there you are laughing at life's maladies felt

You remind me of my mother, no complaining needed
For your faithful love is so deep and growth seeded
Your soul mystical, yet so evident in a heart's feeding

May this day of a special birth, be of spirited joy

For I thank God for your specialty for this little boy
Your loving friendship will be honored, ship ahoy

A Splendid Birthday Wish.
Love's Friendship
Burkie

"My Heart"

I write about her most every day
I dream of her every blessed night
I see her in my vision in every way
She is within my heart, my delight

She's away from me this very moment
Yet, so strong within my very soul
Capturing this man's amazing torrent
Knowing I am so complete and whole

No matter distance, she is here within
Her warmth flows through me as the sun
Worshiping her words of love, once again
Returning to me after her days of fun

Heaven is very contented, even while away
For the moments will soon be replenished
She will appear again within a splendid day
Knowing our love will never be diminished

You are always within My Heart of Love. Robert'

"Sailing Within My Heart"

You have me sailing with the emotion of thirst

Here in my mind, the magic rehearsed

As if a play being acted out in life

You drifted within my mind's eye

Living under the splendor of a soft blue sky

You bring my thoughts to such pleasure

When I envision your goodness I so treasure

Your spirit, your inspiration for others

Who share your specialty, being a profound lover

Yes, I thirst for such sustenance here

Within your arms of splendor, my dear

Creating inspiration for others, not fear

I thank the Lord, I took the chance

For now, I know the splendor of dance

Emotions and visions capture my heart

I knew of the wind's direction from the start

For the sails fluttered with such bliss

Under the stars and moon, a heavenly kiss

Love, Robert

"We cannot direct the wind, but we can adjust our sails"

"Love"

I visualize my arms enveloping you within the softness of still water

Caressing the Voice of God's blesses tide so near to our senses

As His moon and stars captured our hearts as one, forever

I remember the peace I felt within your heavenly kiss

Far different than my many prior years of living without you

I felt the serenity of true goodness without feeling ordinary

As you held my embrace as an everlasting and loving testament

Of youthful days of laughter and the remembrance of goosebumps

A rebirth of imaginary dreams of splendor as when a perfect child

My heart fluttered, as I tasted the warmth of your body within me

As my breath consumed all of my energy, loves true divinity

God provided His consummated and enlightening passage to life

For you captured every fiber of my human existence in its entirety

On that splendid evening within our only destination in life

The wine of love consumed me to the poets' laurels of romantic history

All the Love within me,
Robert

"Loving You is so Damn Easy the Candle is Lit"

Loving you is so very natural and serene as breathing
Hearing you voice keep my heart profoundly beating
Seeing you before me allows my perfect passion of dreaming
Inhaling your perfect scent has sent me far beyond feelings

Touching you titillates every one of my intricate senses
Caressing you removes all my frailties and human defenses
Your soft alluring whispers loving words enlightens my lenses
Seeing all the world clearly through you leaves me defenseless

Listening to your voice soothes me to the depth of my soul
Hearing your sweet laughter makes my life perfectly whole
I feel your beauty and sweetness within our embrace takes hold
Seeing how fortunate your love is for me, from God, I am told

Watching you while I feel you hearing the musical lyrics
Looking deep within your soft alluring eyes, I see your spirit
Seeing peace and tranquility. I know I feel every part of it
Loving you, a blessing I wanted for years, the candle is lit

Warmest of Love's Possibilities, Forever, Robert

"Love in The Keys"

The soft, tranquil ocean shall bring such devotion
As if God has willed His magically loving potion
Within our hearts, such serenity largely unknown
As others search forever, yet only sigh and bemoan
We shall love lustfully, yet softly within Heaven's place
Where a sunshine can whisper sensual love today
Within the heart of an earlobe, words will only sway
The love beyond universes, stars, and Luna's poetry
In giving our oneness of spirit, a loving sensual oratory
As terns and plovers shall know our name as Love
As we grace our special place, as if finding Heaven above
Seashells of hearts shall speak symbols of our Love
As music and dance shall always offer the song of doves
Where she shall fly of delicately tender butterflies
Traveling to our destination where our spirit exceeds the skies

All the love God can will, so tenderly,
My Beautiful, Sensuous Butterfly.
Robert'

"Imagination"

Expressing love to you expands all the words of expression
Our body and soul express our loving devotion
Words cannot express our loving actions from above
Imagine my loving eyes upon you, awakening
Dancing within our world of natural beauty
Never doubt my love, for you possess it all
Within your eyes I see beyond the realm
Your love brings me to another hemisphere
Where moons and constellations are within view
I lose myself within life, I am born again, renewed
You travel within me, I am a new spirit
Love of a child, loving life's appearance
Waiting days to know such tranquility
Save your imagination for our splendid journey
And, keep your heart strong in our beliefs
Your heart will capture the essence, doubts removed

Love,
Robert

"I am Blessed with Her Love"

I am blessed with her love within my vision
I dream of her love penetrating my lasting decision
To love with the completeness of one's heart and soul
To understand truth of God's love that she forever holds

To know the symbols of lavaliere surrounding her neckline
Of the preciousness her heart gives to me, so well defined
Her heart of an angel, giving all of herself with love
How honored I am for this love from a spirit above

Her eyes have opened that secret window of her spirit
I see so clearly her love when I am simply near it
Her rapture transporting my mind to her rare beauty
Seizing my heart with the care of honor and duty

I am blessed by her love within all of love's expressions
When she is within the soul of my heart's confessions
She is the ray of light within God's infinite plan
Radiating such goodness of love within God's hand

I Love You with all of My Heart and Soul's Symbols, Robert

"Bless This House" (an Irish Poem-author unknown)

Bless this house, O Lord we pray
Make it safe by night and day
Bless these walls so firm and stout,
Keeping want and trouble out
Bless this roof and chimney tall,
Let the peace be over all
Bless the doors that they may prove
Ever open to joy and love
Bless the windows shining bright
Letting in God's heavenly light
Bless the hearth a-blazing there
With smoke ascending like a prayer
Bless the people here within
Keep them pure and free from sin
Bless us all, that one day, we
May be fit O Lord to dwell with thee

Author: Unknown

"Love is Patient"

Author: The Bible: 1 Corinthians 13:4

Love is patient, love is kind
It does not envy, it does not boast
It is not proud,
It is not rude, it is not self-seeking
It is not easily angered,
It keeps no records of wrongs,
Love does not delight in evil,
But rejoices with the truth,
It always protects, always trusts,
Always hopes, always perseveres,
Love never fails.

"Teddie's Love"

Teddie, now running within the heavens' universe

With a healthy young body and a soul fully immersed

A sweetness to other heavenly creatures, he'll find

For the love and affection, he fully displayed in earth's time

Teddie will wag his tail with such pride once again

As he frolics with memories of his family within

His heart will bring the spirit of love to all

And, The Good Lord will know to give him a new red ball

Where he can continue to spread his warmth to every soul

Run Teddie, run as far as the Lord takes you

Knowing we loved you each day we were with you

The Lord's gift to us, born on October 3, 2006

Our gift returned to The Lord on June 6, 2015

Chapter Four

Reflections of Love Lost for The Last Time

About ten years ago now, I experienced my last love affair! It ended as quickly as it started, and I wrote a very good manuscript, entitled, "The Once in a Lifetime Love Affair." Yet, I never published the manuscript. The poems in the previous chapter were poems from this manuscript.

It was a very exciting period of my love life, and for some strange reason in ended in up in court, where I had to defend myself from this former lover's accusations of stalking. The female judge dismissed the case, and now my fear was just how someone, who I shared my most intimate thoughts with could do such a dishonest thing.

I gave up on the future potential of any romantic relations, and surrounded myself with good friends, many females, who I had known for years. These people I trusted, and I had just about enough of people who were either closet alcoholics, or drug addicts. Especially people who came from disturbed families of abuse.

I was now at a new place of peace in my life, and shared great times with old friends. And I began reflecting upon what time I had left in my life, ever so grateful for God's Blessings, knowing that My Ma was now closer to me than any time of my life. I should have been dead at the age of nineteen, from a horrific car accident while in service to my country. Yet, God decided to intervene, and blessed my future. Would I have ever expected to live to my age.... not on your life.

My whole life, I have felt blessed, then besmirched, and blessed again, where My Ma won many a battle on my behalf, along with Gramma and Grampa, who were my surrogate parents for the first years of life. I miss them more so today, especially where I hope to be rejoining them, as I never, ever expected to be of this earth for so long.

I so look forward to my eventual demise, yet so very few have the chance to impart ole style values to the general reader. I realized a long time ago that God blessed me with a talent, that may be my legacy. I hope that my poems may in some way affect your very own spirit, and the value of experiencing a life where one can value life, no matter the obstacles. Especially the new generations, who I hope to impart the majesty of God in one life, especially God's Natural World, not manmade.

I leave the next chapter of poems to express God's Grace.

"I Loved Her, I Feel Her, God I Loved Her"

I loved her because she changed my perspective of Life

I feel her because she is gone to her plight

I loved her for the flame she created within me

I feel her because I am drowning in an emotional sea

I loved her for all the magical moments she gave

I feel her because I loved her in so many ways

I loved her softness within our candlelit bed

I feel her because hurtful words were said

I loved her for the magic truly felt by the ocean

I feel her for the grasp she holds without devotion

I loved her for her vision piercing my mind

I feel her for she is but, one of a kind

I loved her for all the wonderful, joyful tears

I feel her because my heart is no longer here

Love Lost.
Robert

The Sun reflects upon the ocean's waves, a vessel

Traveling within God's time here upon you within His light

He has protected and guided your voyage toward peace

Knowing you have such uniqueness in human spirit

He has nourished you're being since birth as a seedling

Measured the growth of goodness and love within you

He has given you the vision of intricacies unknown to most

Enhanced you're senses to height of the heavens' skies

With the awareness of the simplicity of life's purpose

He is the vessel upon the waves of one's history of life

May you have a blessed and peaceful Christmas with Reflection

Friendship,

Robert

I walk the beach alone within my own turmoil

Knowing I have lost her now, maybe forever

I just wish for our return to each other's hearts

Where a life of trust in love's eternity existed

When the true belief in honor was gallantly accepted

Where everything worth living for was so very possible

I contemplate the efforts of my tears, unending

Hoping to have God give me back my spirit

I am now a lonely wave trapped in the engulfing sea

Where sunshine and blue skies burn my senses

Knowing her soft cloud is at a very far distance

The spark of my life within her has lost its vigor

Her belief that I was more than a pretender of dreams

My thoughts now of her glazers, tears of remembrance

Knowing I shall never touch her heart again

I dream of a new and enlightening day renewed

Whence the loving trust can conquer all and more

Yet her joy now, can only be remembered from afar

As I slowly perish, knowing her belief in me is gone

"Moments Fleeting"

Laughing at life, the fool's mistakes

Attempting to think of a moment's smile

Where pleasant thoughts appeared, once again

Ah, youthful imagination captures my sense of years

While forgetting the upcoming times ahead of me

Oh. But for the radiant beauty she bestowed

Keeps my heart from breaking forever more

It is the sea I now seek with splendid love

For it is here, I envision God's natural beauty

And all of His creatures blessed with delicateness

To the Blessed Years ahead, Happy Birthday

Robert

"Come Home Sweet Children"

When will you be coming Home, Sweet Children,

For Home Sweet Child is here in my Heart

With messages of Love, Peace and Irish Lullabies

Where a vision of my universe are thoughts of understanding

Listen carefully, My Children, understanding is complex

Seek first to understand my nourishing communication

The words will fill your need to believe what is Truth

To see perspective, Life's lesson of Wisdom

The Human Condition always passes with Time

Be graceful in analysis, things are never what they appear

Life and its many challenges offer opportunity to grow

It is never too late to rise above that which challenges

Serious battles are never won, the journey may be impossible

When praise and blame are humbling Life's Lessons

Contentment in your life is the Childhood Kindness given

That remains the knowledge of your goodness today

Upbringing with kindness and goodness are aspects of your life

The simple act of forgiveness exposed you both to wisdom

Having the perspective and introspection to know True Love

Look beyond the battlefield. Comfort the wounded

Know the Cry of Compassion, the Beauty of Human Spirit

Share in the joys of our lifetime together, goodness will prevail

Being right or wrong brings no sense of inner peace

Knowing our life on earth gives no absolute guarantees

Our Love will live forever, not the headstone of a gravesite

So, listen carefully My Loving Children; the message is clear

I Love you with All My Heart, the Heart of Teddy Bear

All My Love & Affection.

Dad

Not one of these Poems to Laura and Kristina ever reached their eyes, as with all of their Teddy Bears who were all placed within plastic garbage bags in Grandma's cellar never to be seen again. God Forgive such despicable behavior to two innocent children, from the ages of 7 years old and 4 years old. Till the present day now at the of 37 years and 34 years. This is the tragedy of "Parental Alienation Syndrome", Which the entire media of Boston ignored during the Deadbeat Dad Crusade of the 1990's till today, all because it is a Custodial Mother's issue, and god forbid it would be exposed within public purview. It took a group of Canadian psychiatrists to bring it to light, yet smothered by U.S. Media and well-known political cronies with the Commonwealth of Massachusetts. Led by a very corrupt 1st Justice of The Middlesex Probate and Family Court. Please refer to two books, the first, "Poems and Letters from Deadbeat Daddy" and a sequel recently published, entitled "Children's Injustice."

Chapter Five

Reflections of Life in Honor of Love & Friendship

Life's experiences should be of value within one's faith, where one sees the frailties and mistakes as a teaching lesson; a chance to help others, particularly true friends with the wisdom I have learned over many years.

I was sometimes placed in situations, as never expected and I used these experiences to see a completely different perspective as to trying to find the underlying reasons for behaviors and deep seeded issues that caused the dilemmas.

What I have learned without any scientific evidence to back up my philosophy, is that people's character is tested, and who we emulate in our childhood often determines our later decisions.

I had the blessing of two phenomenal people, Helen and Henry, known as Gramma and Grampa and an entire family known as the Horgan Family, who I was raised by during my upbringing. They were the funniest people on earth at the time, and I do not remember a moment of sadness, even at a wake or funeral, as they loved everyone. Laughter was the healing balm, and stories were told in remembrance, along with music from an old vacuum pump piano with piano rolls or Grampa or Aunt Agnes playing ole songs while everyone sang the melody and words.

Today, at the ripe age of 74 years, when I think back to these times of joy and heartache, I can actually play a movie in my visual senses, actually being at the scene, as if it was, in fact transpiring today.

The longer I live, the more intricate are the scenes. And the story of Ma (Mom) is written in almost every book I have ever written, because she was the most remarkable woman, I had the privilege of being her Son.

These stories of yesteryear could not happen today, because it was a far different era of life in America. Yet over the past thirty years I have searched for friendly characters in my life, who still believe in honesty, integrity, old morays and folkways, yet I have found very few. Yet those that I have searched out over many years, remain my friends. Many others have disappointed me, yet as my Grampa used to say;

"The number of true friends you will find in life, you can count on one hand, and cut off three fingers"

Well, I am so fortunate to have three steadfast friends, and as I subconsciously plan for my exit from this world, leaving what little I have financially to one friend, and to the children and grandchildren of two friends.

For the reasons of the Grandchildren is their parents were raised old school of principals, and where Family is the cornerstone of Love and Dedication, far above the principles of today. There are certainly benefits of today's global economy, yet it often leads to the detriment of family, where often the family unit is no longer the strength above all else.
In my own story, I wish this were in fact true, yet it is not, and I leave the reader to read the books as to why.

Esther, Rosemary, and Paul, I so thank you for bestowing the honor of being your friend.

Please reader. allow me to thank you for interpreting my Poems of Friendship.

The Sun reflects upon the Ocean waves, a vessel

Traveling within God's time here upon you within His light

He has protected and guided your voyage toward peace

Knowing you have such uniqueness in human spirit

He has nourished you're being since birth as a seedling

Measured the growth of goodness and love within you

He has given you the vision of intricacies unknown to most

Enhanced you're senses to height of the heavens' skies

With the awareness of the simplicity of life's purpose

He is the vessel upon the waves of one's history of life

May you have a blessed and peaceful Christmas with Reflection

Friendship,

Robert

"Thoughts of Our Love"

I sit within my solitude of Crane's Beach

On an early morning in May, completely alone

Except for you, embraced here within my Heart

The Sun glistens upon our crystal sands

As migrating birds circle my place of refuge

The breeze is softly caressing all of my visual senses

I sit with you between my legs, your back against my chest

I kiss the back of your sweet neck

I feel your warmth against me, I smell your perfect scent

Oh, how I wish I could physically hold you so close

To find my peace and share your truest happiness

Let no human journey within our spot today, God's gift to us

The Sun becomes God's warmth upon my inner being

And, I smell His nature's gift of the tranquil sea

I feel the dunes and soft waves envelop me

The wind spreads its fingers upon the sparkles of sand

I can feel your hand caressing mine, the touch of your spirit

And, we find our visual senses of beauty within God's paradise

A place on Earth where we are only left to our thoughts

And, our love of the ocean's coast of beauty and tranquility

You, so understand my Love for this place on Earth

Where humans have not embarked upon its true beauty

For it is here in my solitude that I am with you

Feeling such Love, comfort and excitement of all our senses

I know the Lord blessed me by bringing you

To my life of splendor, feeling all your thoughts and senses

I Love you so much, lesser only to the One, who blessed me

Two Stanzas plus two more Stanzas

I often think of my last days
And the thoughts that may amaze
Not of fortune or shameless fame
But of simple kindness
Of simple laughter's goodness
A gracious caress, I must confess

I wonder the peace attained
The memories that sustained
The sights of beauty remained
My friend, the ocean's blue
Shall wave the past I knew
A journey to be reviewed

Poetry left behind from the heart
Childhood memories, many a laugh
Romances and love so far apart
Flight of wings to other universes
Magical moments, no rehearsals
Life passed to celestial verses

Plovers and terns surround my ashes
Warming sands, ocean's passage
Whispering clouds, soft breeze dashes

Above the remaining earth below
Life was meant to bestow
Love and Friendship all in tow

"Lost and Found"

As one travels the older version of self
Dreams enhance the message of help
When one returns to visions of beauty
Laughter and peace become perpetuity
I understand the simplest of kindness
Distain disappears, heartfulness is now near
A sonnet, a play, real poetry now reappears
Where magic once lived, the scent of love
A lustful kiss, heavenly bliss from above
It sustains me, a dance in the heavens
Sky writing, cloud full images of clear heavens
A lightness of mind, a vision of bond
Where soft touches of the soul are found

Peacefulness in Place.

Robert

"Reflections of Love"

I have no understanding, no forgiving thoughts
We found what others only wished for
Caresses of peace and love had found our very heart
Within a life of fleeting moments captured anew

We loved the sea's calming our spirit
Consumed within our transformation
We lusted for the thirst of youth
Simply blessed with the truth of transparency

You brought us belief without fear
As time was urgent to capture the sun
Within a universe you sought for me
My eyes saw such a radiance of God

I felt not worthy of such blessings
Nothing ages quicker than happiness
For our paths converged without words
Lost within life's true direction

I returned to the ocean's serenity
To seek myself and reflection

In contemplation of love's truth
Knowing all of God's true blessings

I found my love for her of such perfection
All fear unraveled and was cast away
Forever, the love of one's lifetime
Traveled beyond my human stay

God spoke to me within her touch
The scent of perfect sensual lust
Where love had not been truly known
Until she became my life's vision and trust

I shall never doubt again, not for a moment
For she is now imbedded within my soul
Her goodness reflected within my heart's truth
She is forever the meaning of being whole

I will never know the word, forsake
For her tears of joy have pieced my spirit
With God's truth of love and goodness
Bringing life to its final, blessed conclusion

"Inner Peace"

In Light's dawning hour, the depth of darkness removed

I feel a sense, a purpose of life's true beauty in you

A prayer for the darkness to emit candlelight, a spirit soothed

Where the inner peace reaches the depth of my soul

No longer tormented by mind's pain that existed

Relenting to kindness, caring, love making us whole

Where true knowledge is a capacity without limits

Turning decades of endless search into endless possibilities

Now present in the visions knowing no inhibitions

From the voices of darkness, the conscience known in sleep

Allowing such deep feelings to reach the pinnacle of compassion

Where our minds speak gently, allowing us to reap

The blessings of love that can be so very fulfilling

Through our hearts and our spirit, true to be pure

When we come to this unimagined place, we must be willing

To the commitment of another, truest of love must be secure

"For My Friend, a Birthday Wish"

There are many blessings I want for you

So many wishes in my heart

As I have watched your life unfold before me

I wish the witness of tranquility and peace

I wish you ultimate strength

I wish you sensitive wisdom without refrain

Of adventure and wonderful life experiences

I wish you the serenity within listening

To your inner voice as the earth rushes

Around you with generosity

And the contentment of being loved.

Moments captured and treasured

Cherish my greatest wish,

To always remember the abundance

Of inner beauty and love within you

Happy, Blessed Birthday
Robert (Burkie)

"Happy Birthday Pops"

Another year passes so incredibly fast
What is present today, tomorrow is past
Keep a light shining as long as it lasts

Enjoy life's blessings in the forefront
Laugh at the aches and pains as merely stunts
Remember, not long ago, you were just a runt

Life passes quickly in the blink of an eye
See things more clearly, laugh for being alive
Take time for reading the etchings in the sky

Celebrate unbridled frivolity upon your birthday
Knowing you have been blessed more today
Than all the other that you are here to stay

So, savor the wine, we call the nectar of life
Simplify its meaning above all the strife
Know the love that you give to all, gives twice

Blessed Birthday
Love and Fidelity's Friendship
Robert (Bob)

"Hanukkah Friendship"

There are many people you shall know in one's life
Yet, far few who shall portray the qualities of true friendship
For a special friend exudes laughter in times of strife
While easing the turmoil with kindness and a spirit's kinship
Knowing that life is merely a journey to be reviewed with glee
For we are of this earth for little time to ponder its inequities
No need to fully understand life's parables, enjoy possibilities
For the true friend understands the goodness of heart rendered
Without receipt for fulfillment of good and honorable deeds
It is of a different and far greater emotion than words express
It is of the action within one's constant spirit, heartfelt giving
That is why it is said. 'true friendship lasts forever.'

Have a Precious Holiday
With Friendship.
Robert

"Happy Blessed Birthday"

Happy Birthday, what should that mean to you
Does it mean God loves you from His distant view?
Does He come closer to your heart; whispering thank you?
He knows it's Your Birthday, remember…He created you
And, He silently follows you everywhere you travel in life
Guiding Your Spirit's journey, removing all of the strife
His goal for your future is what keeps you, so alive
He is such a part of your unwavering, incredible drive
To many destinations, He is clearing your charted path
As all of your friends are privileged to share many a laugh
For He has blessed you with Angels of His entire staff
Assigned to protect you, such a precious earthly gift
All of us who know and love you, our hearts you so lift

Happy Birthday
Robert

"God's Holy Name upon Hanukkah"

Always My God for our people of Israel with mercy and love
Pled for our ancestors' cause and executed judgment from above
Avenged the wrongs with righteousness delivering strength anew
You delivered just deliverance and redemption in history's review
Children's achievement from blessed hands, your Holy Torah
Unto a great and holy name in our world of glory's splendor
Our children enter the sanctuary of your purified House
Your Holy Temple with kindled lights, your Holy Court
We appoint these festive eight days as Blessing's purport
We give thanks unto your Holy name, for eternity's word
Our covenant, a solemn vow, always God's Miracle served

My You Hanukkah be festive in celebrating God's Miracle
He is the symbol within the oiled flame's purity of your Menorah.

Loving friendship,
Robert (Burkie)

"A Blessed Christmas"

Despite the times within our world
Christ remains our pillar of strength
He brings out the peace within our soul
No matter the turmoil, no matter the hurt
His story touches us to make things whole
We believe within ourselves through His gospel
He remains a messenger while we inhabit this earth
Of good conscience and deeds, forgiveness of offense
It is personal to all of us who live by faith's evidence
To worship with thoughts as all of His Children
His ultimate sacrifice planned since His birth
The Son of God sent to us to teach us of life
To understand our path to His ultimate Universe

A Very Blessed Christmas
Loving Friendship
Robert

"This Day, a Wish"

May today be blessed within your heart
Your subliminal thoughts of love a part
Of celebration from it's very brilliant start

Make today a journey in awakening all senses
From your inception at birth uniquely extensive
To me, you have magically made love pensive

Hard to accomplish in this day and age's time
Yet, you always see and understand human rhyme
And obstacles are merely challenges in our mind

Your spirit unique, your kindness in giving of self
Cannot usually be found in novels of spirit's wealth
Yet, there you are laughing at life's maladies felt

You remind me of my mother, no complaining needed
For your faithful love is so deep and growth seeded
Your soul mystical, yet so evident in a heart's feeding

May this day of a special birth, be of spiritual joy

For I thank God, for your specialty for this little boy
Your loving friendship will be honored, ship ahoy

A splendid Birthday Wish. Love's Friendship

Robert (Burkie)

"Happy, Happy Birthday"

Another year celebrating life
A healthy spirit as Mother and Wife
True life's blessings renew
Laughter and joy surround you
As the path each year is amazing

May all of your wishes come true
Blue skies, tranquil seas be with you
The Good Lord's blessings abound
As you continue the journey around
A world of laughter and joy

Enjoy the simple moments each day
Finding joy in each and every way
Your goodness of heart cherished
No matter how it is measured
Your life's fire is always blazing

A Blessed Birthday with Friendship.
Robert

"Thanksgiving's Friendship"

There are many people you shall know in one's life

Yet, far few who shall portray the qualities of true friendship

For a special friend exudes laughter in times of strife

While easing the turmoil with kindness and a spirit's kinship

Knowing that life is merely a journey to be reviewed with glee

For we are of this earth for little time to ponder its inequities

No need to understand life's parables, enjoy the possibilities

For the true friend understands the goodness of heart rendered

Without receipt or need for fulfillment of an honorable deed

It is of a different and far greater emotion than words express

It is of the action within one's constant spirit's heartfelt giving

That is why it is said, "true friendship lasts forever."

A Thankful Thanksgiving
With Friendship
Robert

The holidays enlighten the Soul's desire

Breathing the essence of Life, Spiritual Consciousness

Yet, the New year devours the committed Spirit

As mundane Commercialism takes hold of our vestige

An enlightened few see Life ever, so clearly

Imparting Life's true meaning of personal sustenance

I have been Blessed in witnessing your daily presence

Knowing your goodness of Heart and my spirit it penetrates

Clear to my mind's eye, a reflection of enlightenment

Your spirit removes chaos, your touch removes confusion

Your Peacefulness provides Contentment, Insight, Fulfillment

A true Gift from your treasured Heart, influencing Creativity

The Lord blesses my Spirit, having you within my life

You have influenced my Spiritual Path beyond Humanity

You enhanced my search for Wisdom within God's Universe

You are a Great Soul, creating a New Spirit every day

You will always be remembered as the Sage of My Heart

You care for my Inner Spirit, My Essence, My Sustenance for Life

Love, Peace & Friendship in Fulfilling All of Your Desires

Robert

"Thanks Giving"

I thank God for blue skies tapestry
I thank God for the music's rhapsody

I thank God for the willow's delicacy
I thank for the constellation's majesty

I thank God for the moments I consume
I thank God for the spirit of strength renewed

I thank God for spectacular sunlit sandy beaches
I thank God for all the wisdom of love He teaches

I thank God for the spectrum colors of a rainbow
I thank god for wild flowers and pastel bows

I thank God for the rhythm of ocean waves
I thank God for the souls that He saves

I thank God for reflective poetry and prose
I thank God for the righteous path He chose

I thank God for the scents that abound my senses
I thank God for the sounds of laughter's defenses

I thank God for storytelling and parable voices
I thank God for His measure of life's choices

I thank God for perfect perspective, His universal view
I thank God, above all else, for bringing me you

A Blessed & Loving Thanks Giving
Robert

"Thanksgiving"

Thank you for allowing me my freedom of thought
Bringing me such contentment, I've so long thought
Giving freely of yourself without any regret
Living a happy smile since the day that we met

Thank you for understanding my mind's complexity
Accepting my silly ways, my spirit's dexterity
Knowing my frailties, my inner demon's eye
Caring, no matter the difficulties gone bye

Thanks for feeling my emotions, my strength for life's living
For your strong, sensitive spirit, your love of giving
My ways of heartfelt expression leaving words less said
Knowing the love, we feel within the warmth of our bed

Thank you for our communications, far exceeding sexuality
For sending us to our place of splendid sensuality
Giving so much of yourself in one's spirit so felt
Feeling all that you feel, consumed as our hearts melt

Thank you for missing me through all of my principles
Kissing me, showing you care, feeling love is invincible

Giving me a sense of peace, God has truly blessed us
Knowing that my love for you is built upon by such a trust

"The Story Teller"

The Story Teller smiled sweetly as she told her story
Her Children of Children witnessed all of her glory
She spoke of joy, she spoke of heartache
Yet, she always spoke with laughter as her fate
She had seen life so differently, she saw around the bend
Yet she carried this laughter with her until the very end
She spoke in parables so her Children could inwardly think
Of life's true meaning, the chain of The Family link
Life's complexities, yet so simple in its meaning
For this love appeared since each child began teething
She described the loss of finding love with many a man
Yet, she knew her destiny's love was more than a plan
It was God's gift, never to be sacrificed for just a man
Her nurture was her sustainable love, the blossoming children
Children of Children listened to the Story Teller's story within
As her heart and soul's laughter portrayed God's infinite win

Happiness always, Special Birthday Wishes
Friendship's Love

Robert ("Burkie")

"The Prayer"

I pray you'll be our eyes, and watch us where we go

And help us to be wise, in times when we don't know

Let this be our prayer, when we lose our way

Lead us to the place, guide us with Your grace

To a place where we'll be so splendidly safe

The light that you give us, I pray we will find the light

And, stay in our hearts, reminding us when the stars align

You are the everlasting star; our faith when shadows fill a day

Lead us to a place of honor, guide us with Your Grace

Give us faith so we will be safe, we dream of a world at peace

A world of justice and hope, grab your neighbors' hand

As a symbol of peace and brotherhood

The strength that you give us, we ask that life be kind

And watch us from above, where everyone finds love

We hope in each soul we find, in and around the soul to love

Let this be our prayer, just like every child to find

Let this be our prayer, guide us with your grace

Give us faith that you've lit inside us, I feel will save us

A Poem derived from a song sung by Celine Deoine, and Andrea Borcelli.
Original lyrics by Carole Bayer Sager

Whether He was the Son of God, or simply a prophet
He walked in His lifetime with men and women of God
His time path was ordained by our earth's history
His parables were his understanding language
Of a man above mere humankind
His gospel from God was truth for humanity
Yet, humans are fleeting from independent thought
As the mass crowd today are the same as Jesus' time
His message was unwavering, no matter the persecution
Yet, we caste judgment upon different beliefs
Or we see the zealots who think they personally know Jesus
Very few remember His word as to His acceptance of all
And His acceptance of the lowly whore or mindless clown
He blessed all, as did John the Baptist.
Yet all of Jesus' flock were easily put to death

"Truth of Love"

The instinct pervades, the history repeats
Memories close in time can bring such defeat
A measure of truth, of character, suspicion, distrust
The heart and emotions in conflict with trust
May honor prevail, gallantry persist
For there is more to love than history's list
A chance for the heart on its mission of mending
At peace in the belief that love, not fear, is never ending
Without the belief in the goodness of fellow man
The message of weakness draws a line in the sand
We must allow the passion of life to foster today
For God is providing a Spirit in guiding our way
This guide is our symbol of goodness and truth
We only need to believe in our message of time
To deliver the ultimate message through love is sublime

"The Earth is filled with Beauty"

Today, I believe in the beauty of the earth
No matter human indignities since birth
A belief in God, not the myth of humans
His natural world of nature, more than humans
I seek the Earth of splendor and peace
Unobstructed by man's greed and the selfish beast
For the natural goodness emits from its wonder
Yet, humans seek only its resources to plunder
While destroying God's true gift for centuries
Far more than man's very penitentiaries
Yet, no matter the cause of human destruction
God rises to fight for its very construction
Nature without man would be blessed and prosper
Yet, today we worship our very ignorance as profiteers

Wishing you a Special Hanukkah
Redirect our rededication to Our World
Loving Friendship.
Robert

Let me arise and open the gate

To breathe the world's warm air along the beach

And, to let love in, and to let out hate

And anger at living with the scorn of fate

To let in life, and let out death

To be grateful for my strength in faith

For the gardeners who have blossomed

The seeds of nurture and love's soul

A harmony between one's soul and life

People who make us happy with peaceful giving

Who have lived introspectively with inner-serenity

A Joyous and Blessed Christmas

Friendship.

Robert

"Why We Have Mothers' Day"

Mothers teach conscious emotional thought

While Dads teach children not to smoke pot

Mothers care about the goodness of heart

Dads give messages of pressure from the start

Mothers have inherited this unbridled magic

Dads warn children lessons of things tragic

Mothers care about a child's wellbeing

While Dads only teach lessons of seeing

They are so different, yet Mothers hold within

For the betterment of family and avoid the sins

Child; never be haunted by things you don't do

As memories of Mom's life are always in mind's view

A child as a grownup loses the chance to speak love

To a Mother once she is with the Angels and Doves

So, live each day and make it Mother's Day

For time is not promised to we children in any way

A Loving celebration to Esther,
Dear Friend, Robert

"As the Sails Diminish"

As the sails diminished from the horizon
She felt a touch upon her heart
Hearing the voice, he is now gone
She visualized his voyage to the horizon
Remembering his sailing through life
Knowing she would not witness his reality again
From the other side of the horizon, they saw the sail
Arising from the distance of life's voyage
Traveling beyond blue skies and tranquil seas
Angels guiding his path far beyond the land and sea
They gathered within the clouds amongst the stars
Singing rejoice for he is on his way

This poem was always meant for you, before I knew Your Love.
Robert

"Awakening to God's Day"

Awake to a new and brighter day
For you are blessed in particular ways
The ability to see and hear the earth
All of God's beauty and your own worth
Within the life that you humbly live
Feeling God's whisper, the wind He so gives
Cleansing the earth, shifting its direction
Bathing us in sunlight's distant perfection
Washing the shores within the Seas' strength
Shifting the earth's time toward a new day spent
Admiring such perfect simplicity God provides
For centuries without deviation of oceans' tides
Being a shiny speckle within God's History of mankind
Is a blessing within our hearts for all of our Time

Author: Robert H, Burke

"Forgiveness"

Forgiveness brings the spirit a deep cleansing
It lifts the storm of gloom upon one's soul
It spreads a free love of human kindness
Unknown until a tide is forced into recession
By Love's human face of kindness, a child's embrace
The Lord speaks through His world of nature
Far more forgiving than human kind
Expressing without words of hate and despair
Giving of perpetual life to a far greater spirit
For World order and respect for fellow man
Yet, we believe in human dominance in the hierarchy
And human differences only tolerated at best
Since Biblical times we have sworn to the sword
To uphold honor, religion and the riches of zealots
Th Lord blesses us with forgiveness beyond human redemption
He teaches compassion although almighty in power
His humility teaches wisdom beyond human compassion
Reflective of higher spirit beyond human comprehension
Yet, He cleanses my soul in my thoughts and my prayers
And teaches the path I have taken in forgiveness
May His teachings enhance our lives on this Good Earth

When a child loves you
For a long, long time
Not just to play with,
But really loves you.
Then you become real.

It takes a long time.

That's why it doesn't
Often happen to people
Who break easily,
Or have sharp edges
Or who have to be
Carefully kept....

Once you are real
You can't be ugly
Except to people
Who don't understand.

From "The Velveteen Rabbit"
By Margery Williams